HEINEMANN GUIDED READERS

UPPER LEVEL

Series Editor: John Milne

Readers at *Upper Level* are intended as an aid to students which will start them on the road to reading unsimplified books in the whole range of English literature. At the same time, the content and language of the Readers at Upper Level are carefully controlled with the following main features:

Information Control   As at other levels in the series, information which is vital to the development of a story is carefully presented in the text and then reinforced through the *Points for Understanding* section. Some background references may be unfamiliar to students, but these are explained in the text. Care is taken with pronoun reference.

Structure Control   Students can expect to meet those structures covered in any basic English Course. Particularly difficult structures, such as complex nominal groups and embedded clauses, are used sparingly. Clauses and phrases within sentences are carefully balanced and sentence length is limited to a maximum of four clauses in nearly all cases.

Vocabulary Control   At upper Level, there is a basic vocabulary of approximately 2,200 words. At the same time students are given the opportunity to meet new words; in most cases, the meaning of new words is clear from their context.

Guided Readers at Upper Level

BARRIE ELLIS-JONES

The Cinema

HEINEMANN EDUCATIONAL BOOKS
LONDON

Heinemann Educational Books Ltd
22 Bedford Square, London WC1B 3HH
LONDON EDINBURGH MELBOURNE AUCKLAND
HONG KONG SINGAPORE KUALA LUMPUR NEW DELHI
IBADAN LUSAKA NAIROBI JOHANNESBURG
EXETER (NH) KINGSTON PORT OF SPAIN

ISBN 0 435 27031 1

First published 1977
Reprinted with corrections 1978

Cover by Chris Gilbert

Filmset in Photon Times 12 pt by
Richard Clay (The Chaucer Press), Ltd, Bungay, Suffolk
and printed in Great Britain by
Fletcher & Son Ltd, Norwich

Contents

NOTE

In this Reader, care has been taken to explain the technical terms in the text either when they first occur or shortly afterwards. Because of this it has not been found necessary to include a glossary.

ONE

INTRODUCTION

Thousands of years ago there was a group of people who hunted and killed animals for their food. These people lived in caves. On the walls of their caves they painted pictures of the animals that they hunted. And they painted pictures of themselves too. They wanted to show how the animals moved and how people moved when they hunted animals. And so they painted a lot of pictures to show all the different movements the animals and the hunters made.

The caves were dark. They needed lights to see the pictures. With a light they could go from picture to picture and see the whole story of a hunt, with all the movements that the hunters made from beginning to end.

Prehistoric cave painting in the caves at Lascaux, France.

We can still see these caves and pictures in Lascaux, a town in France. They tell us that the earliest men tried to show the movement of the real world in pictures.

In 1895, again in France, the two brothers Auguste and Louis Lumière made a machine that they called the cinématographe. It was from this word that we now have the 'cinema'.

For about sixty years the cinema was the most popular entertainment in the world. Then television was invented and soon became more popular than the cinema.

Here we tell the story of the cinema, and its sixty years of greatness. The most popular films came from one place, from Hollywood. Much of the story of the cinema is the story of Hollywood, the story of the American film industry.

It is a story that has a beginning, a middle and, almost, an end. Most of the Hollywood studios that made films for cinemas throughout the world have now closed or make films for television.

Most of the changes in the cinema happened first in Hollywood. The first successful sound film, *The Jazz Singer*, was made there. And so was the first successful colour film and the first wide-screen film too.

The men who lived in the caves near Lascaux painted their pictures with difficulty in those dark places. Perhaps the painter needed the help of someone who stood with a light so that he could see to work.

The man who makes a modern film needs the help of hundreds and sometimes thousands of other people. In Chapters 9 and 10 we see how a modern film is made. We look at the work of the producer. He is the person who must find a story which people want to see. The film begins with him. He must also find the money to make the film. When the film is finished, it is his job to make sure that people see it. If a lot of people see it, the producer earns a lot of money. But there have been many films that have never been shown in cinemas. If his film is not seen, the producer can lose hundreds of thousands of dollars.

The director actually makes the film. He works for months to make something which stays on a cinema screen for ninety minutes. The result of months of work can be seen in minutes, but it can have a powerful effect.

We know that the cinema has helped to change the way people think. It has also changed the way that people behave. Men have smoked cigarettes like Humphrey Bogart or, in England, like Gerald du Maurier. They grew moustaches like Ronald Coleman. Women wore clothes that made them look like Greta Garbo. A film called *Rock Around the Clock* started a revolution in Western popular music. In Britain there was fighting and screaming everywhere it was shown.

The cinema also brought much deeper changes. It gave people a chance to see parts of the world that they had never seen before. It showed them new ways of living. Hollywood has been called 'the dream factory'. Films gave people new dreams. They showed people that life could be different and, sometimes, better. If you want to change your life, you must be able to dream of something different. But the cinema did not give people one dream. It gave them a great many dreams. But dreams are not real, and the things that happen on cinema screens are not real either. And so the cinema made people want a better life, but did not show them how they could get it.

Before the cinema, people found their dreams in books. But when the cinema came, people saw many different ways of life and felt them more strongly. And so the cinema made people more dissatisfied than they had ever been before.

People still argue about the changes that the cinema brought to the world. And they will go on arguing. They can only agree that the cinema has changed people.

In this book we do not join in these arguments. Instead, we show briefly what the cinema is. We speak about the different kinds of films that have been made, and about the different people who have made them.

In their caves, the men of Lascaux made pictures of the things that happened in their lives. When we look at these pictures now, they help us to understand the lives of the people who painted them.

Many of the films that have been made since 1895 show the life of the last eighty years. Thousands of years from now, they may still show how people lived in the twentieth century.

TWO

THE BEGINNINGS

One of the early films tells a very simple story. A gang of outlaws ties up a railway telegraph man and holds up a train. The telegraph man is found by his little daughter and set free. He gives the alarm. The Sheriff calls the townsmen together and they ride off on their horses to capture the outlaws. There is an exciting chase and in the end the outlaws are captured.

It is a simple story, but it is a very important one. It is the story of a film called *The Great Train Robbery*, which was written, photographed and edited by an American, Edwin S. Porter, in 1903.

The Great Train Robbery, like many films of the time, was about eight minutes long. It told a story and that was unusual. But it was not the first film to do so. Also, it was a Western, but not the first Western. The real difference between *The Great Train Robbery* and earlier films was that in *The Great Train Robbery* the camera moved. When the horsemen rode past, the camera turned and followed them. They rode downhill and the camera moved down and followed them.

In the theatre, everything must happen on the stage in front of the audience. Events are brought to the audience. But, by moving his camera, Porter allowed his cinema audience to follow the events. For the first time, a film was telling a story in a new way.

The first cinema performance had taken place in 1895. By that year, inventors in Europe and America had made the first moving picture cameras and projectors. There were many different ones and each machine had a different name. There was the Bioscope, the Bioskop, the Biograph, the Cinématographe and the Cinematoscope, the Kineopticon, Kinetograph, Kinetoscope and the Vitascope.

Edison's laboratory in New Jersey, USA, showing a phonograph and kinetograph.

A scene from the film, *The Great Train Robbery* directed by Edwin S. Porter in 1903.

The inventors made their machines because they believed that moving pictures could be useful to science. They did not dream that their inventions would lead to the greatest entertainment industry in the world.

The first moving pictures were not shown in cinemas on large screens. They were shown on little screens in machines called Kinetoscopes. Only one person at a time could look into the machine to see the film.

The Kinetoscope was invented in America in the early 1890s by an Englishman, W. K. L. Dickson. He worked for the great American inventor, Thomas Edison. Edison had asked him to make a machine which would show moving pictures. The idea was to combine this machine with Edison's phonograph, the first gramophone. Dickson's first film showed Dickson talking while his words could be heard on the phonograph. And so the first film was a sound film. But it was difficult to show the film and play the sound exactly together. Because of this, Dickson's Kinetoscopes were sold without sound.

Inventors in Europe were able to learn from the Kinetoscope. In a short time France, England and Germany had their own machines. The Frenchmen, Auguste and Louis Lumière, showed their first films throughout Europe in the years after 1895. Their machine was called the Cinématographe and by the end of 1896 they had sent it to India and Australia. In 1897 it reached Japan. And so, from the very start, the cinema was international.

The first films were a great success with the public. They were shown in theatres, small halls and in fairground tents. Audiences sat crowded on hard chairs to see them. A favourite film showed a train rushing towards the audience. When it was first shown, the people in the front rows jumped up and ran.

These early films were a new toy. Those made by the Lumières often showed the street outside the hall in which the audience was sitting. People saw on the screen the outside world that they had just left. And they thought that it was wonderful, even though the world on the screen was in black, white and grey. The audiences were delighted to watch grey waves rolling onto grey beaches for a minute at a time. These films usually lasted for only one minute. And there were pictures of circus acts, little pieces of theatre plays, visits by foreign statesmen and military parades. But after a time the audiences became bored with these films.

It was another Frenchman, Georges Méliès, who first saved audiences from boredom with their new toy. Méliès had seen the Lumières' first show in Paris in December, 1895. He was a magician and immediately thought of using films in his stage show. The Lumières were friends of his and he asked them to sell him one of their Cinématographe machines. But they refused. So Méliès went to London, where a man called Robert Paul was making machines of his own. Méliès bought the English machine and returned to Paris.

Méliès soon discovered the magic possibilities of trick photography. While the Lumières were still showing street scenes and parades, Méliès was making people appear and disappear in his films. It was a simple trick. He stopped the camera and moved the actor in front of it. Then he started the camera again.

He also invented the technique of the dissolve. In a dissolve, one scene slowly changes to the next without any sudden jump. Méliès did this by winding back the film in his camera a little way at the end of one scene. Then he filmed the beginning of the next scene over the end of the one before.

Méliès did most of his filming in a small studio just outside Paris. It was in this little studio that he made his most famous film, *A Voyage to the Moon*. Moon explorers are shot at the moon in a shell from a gigantic gun. We see the shell flying through the air and hitting the Man in the

Moon in the eye. After they land on the moon, the explorers leave their gun-shell. They see the earth rise above the moon's horizon and meet moon monsters.

The film is both clever and funny. Méliès had shown that films could do more than simply show things moving. And throughout Europe and America other film-makers quickly learned this lesson. Even the Lumières began making films that told simple little stories. Films had become more than a toy.

But when we look at Méliès' films today, we can see that there is something missing from them. And the thing that is missing is the moving camera. In spite of all Méliès' trick photography, his inventiveness and humour, his films look flat. For Méliès, the camera was like the audience in a theatre. The camera stayed still and he made all his events happen in front of it. When we see his films, we feel that we are in a theatre.

But, when people saw *The Great Train Robbery*, they knew they were in a cinema. As soon as Edwin Porter moved his camera, they knew they were seeing something different. It is a simple dramatic story, told without any trick shots, but it is something no theatre could ever show.

Audiences loved *The Great Train Robbery* and it was a great financial success. Its technique was copied at once by other American film-makers and in England, two years later, by Cecil Hepworth. This was in a film called *Rescued by Rover*. In this film the camera not only moves, but at times it shows the world from the eye-level of its hero, the dog Rover.

But the style of *The Great Train Robbery* was not copied by everybody. Méliès, for example, never used it. Even Porter himself did not always use it afterwards. And four years later, in 1907, a company was formed in Paris which deliberately made films of a very theatrical kind. This was the *Film d'Art*. It filmed classical plays and used famous stage actors. The films that it produced were nothing more than plays without sound. These films succeeded in attracting an educated audience. The *Film d'Art* did not succeed, however, in making films into a form of art.

THREE

THE BIRTH OF HOLLYWOOD

For the first twenty years of the cinema, no one country was more important than any other.

In France, there was Georges Méliès, who was popular throughout the world. There were films of chases and the comic films of Max Linder. And, of course, there was the *Film d'Art*.

In Britain, James Williamson in *Fire* and Cecil Hepworth in *Rescued by Rover* introduced new film techniques such as editing and the tracking shot.

Later, in Italy, spectacular epics were made, beginning with Luigi Maggi's *The Last Days of Pompeii*. Giovanni Pastrone used about eight hundred actors in *The Fall of Troy* and there was Enrico Guazzoni's *Quo Vadis?* and Pastrone's *Cabiria*. All of them were internationally popular films.

Films slowly became longer. First there were the one-minute films of the Kinetoscope and of the Lumières in the 1890s. Then in the 1900s there were films like *The Great Train Robbery* and *Rescued by Rover* which lasted eight to ten minutes. By 1910, the *Film d'Art* films were almost as long as modern films and some Italian epics were even longer.

In America, films were shown in theatres called Nickelodeons. The audience sat on hard chairs or wooden benches and the entrance fee was very small. The Nickelodeons showed programmes of five or six films, and each film usually lasted for about fifteen minutes.

A company called the Motion Picture Patents Company tried to control the making of all films and all the Nickelodeons in the USA. The company was formed in 1908 by the nine biggest film companies of the time. They worked in New York and Chicago. It was partly because of the activities of the Motion Picture Patents Company that Hollywood became the film capital of the USA.

The Motion Picture Patents Company was the only company allowed by the law to make films, cameras and projectors. But America is a large country and film companies that did not belong to the MPPC decided to work in California.

California was a good place for film companies. The weather was good in winter with enough daylight to film in, and taxes were lower than in New York or Chicago.

Between 1910 and 1915 most American film companies moved to California and these independent companies became more successful than the MPPC. A suburb of the town of Los Angeles became a popular place for the film companies to build their studios. Mack Sennett built his Keystone Studios there and made one hundred and forty short comedies in his first year. Thomas Harper Ince made Westerns with William S. Hart and some fifty real Indians nearby at Inceville. There was plenty of sunshine, with sea and mountain, desert and farmland nearby. And the name of this Los Angeles suburb was Hollywood.

A third studio was linked with Keystone and Inceville. The three together formed a company which called itself Triangle. The third studio was called Mamaronek and was run by the man who made the cinema into a form of art.

His name was David Wark Griffith.

Before 1910, Griffith had been a young actor who wanted to become a writer. He took a film script to Edwin S. Porter, who was then the head of the Edison Company. Porter did not use Griffith's script, but gave him the leading part in a Western called *Rescued from the Eagle's Nest*.

Griffith did not stay long with Porter and the Edison Company. Some of his scripts were bought by another company, American Biograph. Soon Griffith was directing films for Biograph, which became for a time the most successful of all the American companies.

Biograph was a leading member of the Motion Picture Patents Company and made films for the Nickelodeons. Because the Nickelodeons always showed films of about fifteen minutes, Biograph would not make longer films. Griffith was not happy about this.

In 1911 he made a film called *Enoch Arden* which was thirty minutes long. Biograph showed it in the Nickelodeons in two parts. Then, in 1913, Griffith made an hour long film called *Judith of Bethulia*. He knew that Biograph would not agree to the length and he made the film secretly in California. When it was finished, Biograph were not interested in it and refused to let Griffith direct another film.

Griffith left Biograph and took with him his cameraman, Billy Bitzer. He also took with him the actors that he had trained over the years. Griffith had filmed the faces of these actors in close-up. He had done this in spite of Biograph's belief that nobody wanted to see half an actor. Biograph felt that audiences were paying for the whole actor, and so all of the actor should be shown on the screen.

Griffith went to Hollywood in 1913. There, he formed his own studio called Mamaronek which became part of the Triangle Company. Now he was able to make pictures

A scene from *Birth of a Nation* directed by D. W. Griffith in 1914.

of any length he wanted, and the following year he made *The Birth of a Nation.*

Since 1912, American audiences had been able to see Italian and French epic films. They were much longer than American films and had a larger number of actors. Guazzoni's *Quo Vadis?* was shown in New York in 1913. It was twice as long as Griffith's *Judith of Bethulia.* Even so, *The Birth of a Nation* was daring in its length because it lasted three hours. Griffith had the music specially written for a full orchestra. The effect of the film was enormous. The President of the USA, Woodrow Wilson, had the film shown to him in the White House. After the showing, the President said: 'It's like writing history in lightning.'

The story of the film was about the American Civil War and life in the Southern States in the years after the war. The villains of the story were negroes and the heroes were the white men of the Ku Klux Klan. It was a story that caused a great deal of argument, and so a great many people went to see the film. In a few years it made one hundred and fifty times more money than it had cost to make.

But the importance of *The Birth of a Nation* lies in the way the story was told. It was cinema at its best. In the many films that he had made for Biograph, Griffith had been learning cinema technique. He did not invent techniques, but learned the best way to use them. He understood the difference between the cinema and the theatre. This can be seen in the way that he used his camera, in his editing, and in the way that he trained his actors to act. He always preferred to use actors who had not acted in a theatre.

By 1910 the faces of some American cinema actors were well known; but their names were not known at all. This was because the American film companies did not want audiences to know the names of their actors. The

Florence Lawrence, the first 'film star'.

film companies believed that if people knew the actors' names the actors would ask for higher wages. People recognised film actors, of course, and gave them names like 'Little Mary', 'the Biograph girl' and 'Broncho Billy'.

The struggle between the independent companies and the Motion Picture Patents Company brought this situation to an end. Carl Laemmle, the head of an independent company, persuaded the 'Biograph Girl' to leave Biograph and join his company. He gave her more money and let the public know her name; and so, in 1910, Florence Lawrence became the first film star. Although Laemmle had to pay her more, he was also able to charge the cinemas more for her films. Cinema owners knew that a Florence Lawrence film would have a large audience of people who wanted to see her. This first step was successful and other companies soon did the same.

In 1910 good film actors in America earned about 100 dollars a week. Four years later they were earning 2000 dollars. And by 1917, the greatest stars, Charlie Chaplin and Mary Pickford, were earning almost a million dollars a year.

FOUR

SPEECH

The American film industry had started in New York and Chicago. Then, as we have seen, it moved to Hollywood. At the same time it became more and more expensive to make films. This was partly because films were getting longer. The average hour-long film in 1912 had cost about 700 dollars. Griffith's *The Birth of a Nation* cost 110,000 dollars. His next film, *Intolerance*, which was slightly shorter and made a year later, cost a million dollars. The high salaries of the film stars also added to the costs.

The film industries of the European nations were weakened by the First World War. By the end of the war, the American film industry was the biggest and most successful in the world. Hollywood had become the world's film capital.

Film was more real in many ways than the theatre. The camera could go where it wanted to. It could look at a face or a hand, or it could show a whole army on the march. But there were other ways in which it was less real than the theatre. The film screen had no depth. It was not even very wide. Most films had no colour. They were simply black, white and a thousand shades of grey. But most of all, films were silent.

This did not mean that there was no sound at a film performance. Audiences at the Lumière films heard the sound of the projector working.

And there was music too. The smallest cinema had a piano. Some of the big cinemas had full orchestras to play the music for such films as *The Birth of a Nation*. In many cinemas there was a man who made sound effects. When a gun fired on the screen, he made the bang on a drum. When thunder rolled, he rattled an iron sheet.

And so these films were not shown in silence. There was plenty of sound, but there was no speech. In place of speech, subtitles were shown on the screen. The subtitles explained what was happening or what someone was saying. But they broke up the action of the film because everything had to stop while the audience read the subtitles.

Directors of silent films developed extremely clever techniques. Some of these techniques helped the audiences to understand what was happening in a film without the use of words at all. The best directors sometimes used silence to their advantage. But most films suffered badly from their lack of speech.

As we have seen, Edison's Kinetoscope had already joined sound and film together. And quite a number of the very short, one-minute films were made in this way. The sound was played on a phonograph or gramophone and the film was run through a projector. However, it was extremely difficult to show longer films using two separate machines. The sound and the picture often moved at different speeds and so were out of synchronisation – the sound of the words was heard before or after the movement of a person's lips.

An American technician, Lee de Forest, worked on the problem of perfect synchronisation from 1919 to 1924. He was finally successful. He photographed sound waves onto film and ran the film of the sound waves alongside the picture itself. Sound and picture were now joined together. At first, de Forest used his invention on short films and the film industry paid no attention to it.

But in 1926, the Warner Brothers film company was in difficulties. It was not earning enough money. The company looked for something new to make their pictures more attractive. They decided to use sound. But they did not use Lee de Forest's system. Instead they used a system invented by Bell Telephone Laboratories. Huge disc records carried the sound for each reel of film. And so at the end of 1927, Warner Brothers brought out a sound film called *The Jazz Singer*.

The star of this film was the popular singer, Al Jolson. *The Jazz Singer* was such a success that all the other film companies saw at once that they would have to use sound too. And the sound system that the other companies used was sound on film, like Lee de Forest's invention. It is this kind of sound system that is still used for most films today.

Speech had come to the cinema, but nobody knew how to use it. In 1928, the best film directors in Hollywood were the ones who knew how to make very good pictures without speech. And film stars had never needed to have good voices. Actors without good voices suddenly found that they were no longer needed.

New actors with good voices were needed. And so actors from the New York theatres crossed America to Hollywood and were given work in the new talking pictures. These new actors acted in films in the same way as they had acted on the stage. Films began to look theatrical again, like so many of the very earliest films.

There were other, equally important, reasons for this. The cameras which were used to make films were very noisy machines. Huge boxes were built round them to stop the noise getting out. The cameras were trapped inside their boxes and unable to move. Without a moving camera, the films looked like theatrical plays.

They looked theatrical and they sounded theatrical too. This was not surprising, because many of them were written by men who had always written for the theatre. But what is the difference between the speech of the theatre and the speech of the cinema?

The main difference is that the cinema needs fewer words. In the theatre everything happens in a small space, but the audience cannot see small movements. They cannot see the emotions on an actor's face. And so the writer must give words to the actor to explain his emotions. The cinema screen, however, can show us an actor's face and the cinema audience can understand an actor's emotions immediately. If the actor uses words to explain his feelings, the audience becomes impatient. It knows the emotions and does not need the words.

And so, when speech came to the cinema, it brought many new, and old, problems with it. But whether new or old, the problems were similar to the ones which the very first films had brought. Because they were so similar, Hollywood was able to solve them quite quickly.

Speech came to the cinema at a fortunate time. The success of *The Jazz Singer* brought money to Warner Brothers. And the success of the new sound pictures brought money to the whole film industry at a time when money was not easy to earn. Two years after *The Jazz Singer* was first shown in New York, many American businesses were in serious trouble. In 1929 and the years that followed, money was hard to find anywhere. But not in the film industry. Most industries lost money, but the film industry made more money than it had ever made before.

Between 1927 and 1929, the size of cinema audiences in America almost doubled. Hollywood did not suffer the money problems of the rest of the world. The film industry thought that it was safe from everything. They did not believe that the day would ever come when the cinema would not be the most popular entertainment in the world.

FIVE

MONEY, COLOUR AND THE DOCUMENTARY

Money

Sound had made the cinema more popular than ever, and Hollywood was earning more and more money. In the 1930s, America had about 17,000 cinemas. Italy had more cinemas than any other country ouside America, and Italy had only 6,000. Most countries could not make enough films to keep their cinemas busy. So they bought films from America.

Foreign countries bought so many American films that one third of Hollywood's money came from abroad. Because Hollywood earned more money than any other film industry, it was able to spend more money on its films. Because it spent more money on its films, they looked better than anybody else's. Because they looked better, more cinemas around the world showed them. And because more cinemas showed them, they earned more money.

A successful film, shown throughout the world, cost a lot of money to make, but it earned a lot more than it cost. An unsuccessful film also cost a lot of money, but it earned very little, or even nothing at all. And so it was important for the Hollywood film companies, the big studios, to make successful films.

But what was a successful film? Quite simply, it was a film that a large number of people paid money to see. It was not until after the film had been made that the studio really knew if the film was successful or not.

The studios, of course, did all that they could to make sure that their films would be successful. They used stars, because they knew that audiences wanted to see them. And they chose a story like that of their last successful film. And so, throughout the history of the cinema, films have repeated the same kind of successful stories. If someone tried something different and it was successful, then films were made like the new success.

Luckily, audiences liked a lot of different kinds of films. In the late 1920s and early 1930s, for example, Warner Brothers made gangster films. The stories took place in grey city streets. Many scenes happened at night. They were violent films and very close to the life of the real gangsters. These films were very successful.

At the same time, Warner Brothers made musicals. These films were full of songs and dances. They were not like real life at all. In many ways they were the opposite of the gangster films. But these two kinds of films were made in the same years by the same studios. And each kind was as successful as the other.

In the late 1930s, Hollywood was making more films each year than ever before. In later years it made more money, but it never again made as many films so quickly.

28

Colour

The 1920s had seen the coming of sound and the 1930s saw the coming of a successful colour system. The story of colour is longer and more complicated than the story of sound.

Before the first moving picture was made, there had been colour in photographs. The first colour photograph was taken in 1861, more than thirty years before the Lumières invented their Cinématographe.

In 1906, the English film-maker, G. A. Smith, used a system called Kinemacolor. Before that, Méliès and other French directors had painted colour onto their films by hand. Kinemacolor was difficult to use. Painting by hand took a lot of time, did not give good results and was very expensive.

In the early 1920s, colour was used a little. Technicolor produced a system using two main colours. The first film to be made in two colours was *The Toll of the Sea* in 1922. In 1926, the same system was used for *The Black Pirate* and it was also used with sound for *On With the Show* in 1929. But in the 1920s colour was mostly used only in parts of films. Often this was only one colour. Night scenes were printed on blue film, fields and woods were printed on green film, and fire was printed on red film. The colour did not look real, but it was not used in a real way.

It was not until 1932 that Technicolor made a good colour film. This time, instead of two main colours, they used three, and three are still used today. The first film to use the Technicolor three-colour system was *Flowers and Trees*, made by Walt Disney.

Colour was more expensive to use than black and white film, but slowly it was used more and more. Today, films are only made in black and white for special reasons.

Colour became popular far more slowly than sound. If

the colour on the screen was wrong, it annoyed the audience. If the men had purple faces and the women's faces were bright pink, they looked less real than if their faces were grey. And so colour could not become popular until there was a very good colour system.

But once a good colour system had been developed, there were still problems. People felt that films in black and white showed reality. For example, *The Wizard of Oz*, made in 1939, shows a dream, and this part of the film is in colour. But the film starts before the dream, in the real world, and this is shown in black and white.

The critics who wrote about the cinema argued about sound for a short time and then accepted it. But they argued about colour for thirty years. The argument is at last over. Black and white film is still used occasionally, but most of the films we see today are in colour.

The Documentary

The 1930s saw the growth of colour, and they also saw the growth of a new kind of film. The new kind of film came from Britain, not from Hollywood. It was made to tell audiences about the world around them and how other people lived. It was called the documentary film.

In 1922, an Irish-American explorer, Robert Flaherty, went to the far north of Canada to make a film about the Eskimos. It was called *Nanook of the North* and in it Flaherty made the life of the Eskimos into an exciting story. It was not a completely new idea.

Ever since the Lumières, there had been films which showed real life and events. Sometimes news of an exploration made a complete film in itself. One film of this kind was *With Scott to the South Pole* by Cherry Kearton and H. G. Ponting. It was first shown in 1913.

There were also films which showed life in distant places, called travelogues. Films like this taught their audiences about the world. They were educational. In *Nanook of the North*, Flaherty combined education with a story. And he used real people, not actors. It was a great success and he was asked to make another film. This next film was *Moana*. It was about life on a Pacific island and it took him two years to make.

A Scotsman, called John Grierson, wrote about *Moana* in *The New York Sun*, and called it a documentary film. It was the first time that the word 'documentary' was used in this way.

In 1927, Grierson returned to Britain from America and, in 1929, he made a documentary film of his own. Its title was *Drifters* and it described the life and work of Scottish herring fishermen. Grierson believed that the cinema should show people what their fellow-countrymen were doing. Because of Grierson's work, a great many

John Grierson, making the documentary film, *Drifters* in 1929.

documentary films were made in Britain. Throughout the 1930s, there were almost 300 documentary films made on subjects from mining to housing. Even Robert Flaherty went to Britain to make films for John Grierson. And a large number of British film directors learnt how to make films by making documentaries.

When war came in 1939, Britain had film directors who knew how to show real life on film. They continued to make documentaries throughout the war, showing people what was happening in their country and abroad. No one knows exactly how many documentary films were made in Britain during the war, but there were at least a thousand, and they were all made in just under six years.

Some of the directors of documentary films made feature films too. In the documentaries, the directors had learned how to use real people as actors. Now they were able to show actors how to behave like real people. And so their feature films told an exciting story, and looked very real indeed.

SIX

THE COMING OF TELEVISION; THE STAR SYSTEM

The Coming of Television

In 1947, the cinema was the most popular form of entertainment in the world, and had been so for thirty years. But from 1947 onwards, the cinema began to lose its audiences. More and more people, first in America and then in Europe, bought television sets.

One reason why the cinema had become more popular than the theatre was that it was cheaper. Another reason was that it could show far more. It could give audiences something that the theatre could not.

Now television came and provided more entertainment, more cheaply than the cinema. It showed events as they happened and showed them to its audience in their own homes.

Television first became popular in America. Hollywood realised the danger and hurriedly looked for ways of taking people away from their television sets. The cinema had to offer something that television did not have. Colour was one thing. And so more and more films were made in colour.

The cinema screen was, of course, larger than the television screen. But its shape was not very different. And so Hollywood changed the shape of the cinema screen.

A wide-screen system called Cinerama was developed as early as 1952. Three lenses and three rolls of film were needed for every shot in a Cinerama film. One covered the middle of the picture and one covered each side. The film was then shown through three projectors on a very wide screen, and each projector showed a part of the whole picture.

The picture was very large and very wide. The screen was curved, and this gave the audience a feeling of depth. Because the screen was wide and curved, the audience felt that they were inside the events on the screen.

Cinerama was extremely successful, but it was also extremely expensive to make and to show. Cinerama cinemas needed a special screen. They needed special projectors, working three at a time. And they needed a special sound system.

Part of the success of Cinerama came from a new kind of sound — stereophonic sound. There were five loud-speakers behind the huge screen and others at the sides and at the back of the cinema. The sound came from the part of the screen where it was being made. If someone on the left side of the screen was talking, their voice was heard from that side of the screen.

It sounded very real, but it all cost money; more money than most cinema owners wanted to pay. And so the film industry looked for another way of beating television. Their next answer was called Natural Vision, or 3-D.

3-D stood for Three Dimensional. This system used two lenses, which filmed the same scene from slightly different angles. The lenses were set apart just like the two eyes of a human being. Two projectors showed the film and, when the audience looked at it through special spectacles, the picture on the screen appeared to have depth. Depth is the third dimension, and that is why the system was called three dimensional.

Again it was expensive for the cinemas and the spectacles were a nuisance to the audience. Natural Vision was first shown in 1953. It was so unsuccessful that the system lasted only for that one year.

Another depth system was introduced at the end of 1953. It was called CinemaScope. It used a wide screen, like Cinerama, but it was much cheaper. Instead of three lenses and three rolls of film, it used only one special lens and one roll of film. CinemaScope also used stereophonic sound, but with fewer loudspeakers than Cinerama.

CinemaScope was not as powerful as Cinerama, but it was much cheaper. For this reason it quickly became more popular.

The first CinemaScope film was *The Robe*. This was a five million dollar epic which did not rely on wide-screen effects for its success. And, because the film was a success, a large number of cinemas were happy to pay for wide screens and stereophonic sound equipment to show it.

The new wide screen gave problems to the film directors, like every other new technical change. Outdoor scenes were very beautiful, but close-up shots of actors' faces could look ridiculous on a wide screen. But, as before, film directors learned how to avoid mistakes.

The wide screen helped the film industry in its fight against television. The film industry was certainly losing the fight, but it was losing it slowly. Even today, a film star can earn far more money than a television star.

The Star System

In the 1940s and 1950s, the star system was still strong. As we have seen, film stars were not known by name in the USA until 1910. But from that time, the star system grew quickly and remained almost unchanged as part of the film industry until the 1960s.

Most people went to see a film because of the stars in it. And so every Hollywood studio had to have its own stars. Without at least one star, even a good film could be a financial failure. And a bad film could be a financial success because of its stars.

The first film stars – people like Florence Lawrence, Mary Pickford and Charlie Chaplin – were stars because millions of people went to see them. They earned a lot of money and their films were sure to be successful. Every studio wanted these great stars.

Chaplin moved from studio to studio and each time he was paid more money. This was good for Chaplin, but the studios were not happy. They wanted their stars to stay with them, and they wanted to pay them as little money as possible.

To make sure that this happened, the studios employed young and unknown actors under long-term contracts. This meant that the actor agreed to make a certain number of films for the studio. And the studio tried to make the actor into a star.

To do this, the studio had to make its actors and

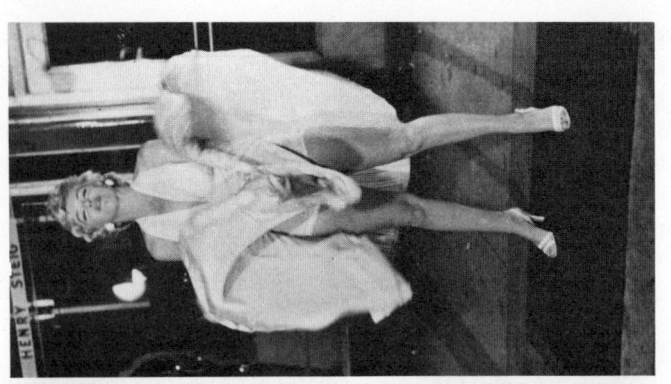

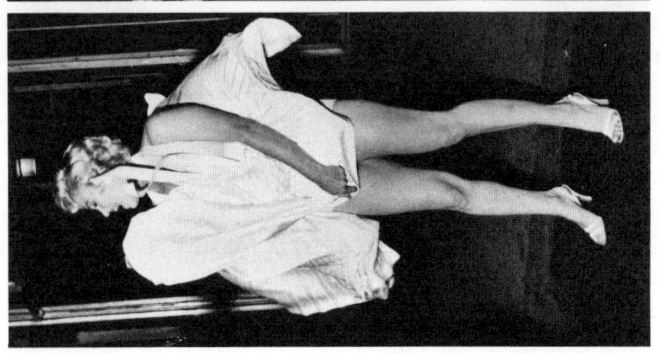

36

actresses known to the public. And the public had to be able to remember them. The actor or actress had to have a name that was easy to remember. It had to be a simple name, but also an unusual one. If the real name of the actor or actress was dull, the studio changed it.

Norma Jean Dougherty was the name of an American actress who went to Hollywood in the 1950s. She had a long, dull name – a name which people could easily forget. And so Norma Jean Dougherty changed her name to one which people could remember. She called herself Marilyn Monroe.

The studios gave their young actors and actresses screen tests. They took some film of them to see what they looked like on the screen. This was very important. People who are very good-looking in real life can look dull on the screen. And some who look dull in real life can look exciting on the screen.

After a successful screen test, the actor or actress was given a part in a film. While the film was being made, the studio tried to interest the public in their new star. They gave pictures and stories of the star to newspapers and magazines so that people knew the star when the film was finished.

Sometimes this worked very well. There were pictures and stories about Raquel Welch in newspapers and magazines before she acted in any film at all. She became a popular film star before she had made her first film.

The studios tried to make stars, but the public decided in the end who really was a star. They did this by going to see the films that the star acted in. The studios knew this very well. They knew that they had to keep trying with a lot of actors before they found a great star.

The star system was a good thing for the studios. It

Opposite: Marilyn Monroe in a scene from the film, *The Seven Year Itch* (1954).

37

saved them money and it allowed them to use their stars as they wanted. It was not such a good thing for the stars. They often had to act in films that they did not like. But the studios did give young actors a chance to become stars. Without the star system, many actors would not have had this chance.

SEVEN

THE 1960s AND THE 1970s

In the 1960s a great many changes took place in Hollywood. The cinemas lost more and more of their audiences to television. And, as we have seen, the cinemas built wide screens and used stereophonic sound to fight television.

For a time, these developments were a help to the film industry, but not for long. Many people had gone regularly to see films and they did not mind whether the film they saw was good or bad. They had gone to the cinema to be entertained. Sometimes they were entertained well; sometimes not very well.

Now these people could stay in their own homes and be entertained by television.

By the late 1950s, Hollywood had a very large number of old films and very few of them were ever shown. Television, particularly in America, needed a lot of programmes to fill up the hours that it was on. The television companies tried to buy old films from Hollywood. At first Hollywood refused. Film companies believed that if people could see films on television, they would never go to the cinema again.

But later, old films became valuable and film companies had to sell them when they needed money. These old films soon appeared on television.

Cinema audiences continued to become smaller and smaller each year. Some people thought that the showing of films on television made the audiences smaller. Others thought that seeing films on television made people want to go to the cinema again. After all, the films on television were often more entertaining than the television programmes.

The star system, which had been so successful in Hollywood in the 1940s and 1950s, began to break down. The stars themselves were dying. In the 1950s, Humphrey Bogart, Gary Cooper and James Dean died; in the 1960s, Clark Gable, Marilyn Monroe, Alan Ladd and Spencer Tracy.

The actors and actresses who took their places did not want to belong to one studio. They wanted to choose the films they were in.

Another cinema institution came to an end in the 1960s. This was the Hay's Office. The Hay's Office had been established in the 1920s and had published a Production Code – a long list of subjects which were not allowed on film. The Hay's Office prevented Hollywood from dealing with human problems in a serious and adult way. Its moral standards were so severe that, by the 1950s, film directors began to fight against them. In 1968, a new and more modern system replaced the old Production Code.

In the 1940s and 1950s, shorter films, called 'B' pictures, were shown in the cinemas with a longer, popular film to fill up three hours' entertainment. These 'B' pictures were usually cheaply made Westerns and were a financial success. In the 1960s, these Westerns were replaced by films showing as many unclothed girls as possible. Films like this were also cheap to make and are now shown in cinemas which show no other kind of film.

Throughout the 1960s and into the 1970s, the Hollywood film companies either closed their studios or sold

A photograph taken of Humphrey Bogart during the filming of *The African Queen*.

James Dean in a scene from the film, *Giant* (1955).

them to television companies.

Television is no longer the enemy of the cinema. Once a film has been seen in the cinemas, television will show it again and again, and will pay to show it. And, in America and Britain, television companies now make feature films of their own.

Even so, fewer films are made. Fewer people go to the cinemas and there are fewer cinemas for them to go to. Television pays to show a film. But the money is much less than a film used to earn in the days when people paid to see it in a cinema.

And so, in the 1970s, we are left with a strange situation. Because of television, more films are seen by more people than ever before. But at the same time, there is less money to make films, and so fewer films are made.

EIGHT

FRENCH, GERMAN AND RUSSIAN CINEMA

The history of Hollywood and the American film industry is the history of the world's most successful film industry. Hollywood made more films which were seen by more people in more countries than any other national film industry. At the height of Hollywood's power, people throughout the world dressed like the Hollywood stars and read stories in their newspapers about the films that Hollywood was making.

Hollywood was an industry, deeply interested in making money. Because of this, and because of the Hay's Office Production Code, people often felt that Hollywood did not make films of any artistic merit. Certainly, a large number of American films paid no attention to art.

Artistic films came from countries outside America and, for many years, chiefly from Europe.

The Hollywood star system sold films by the names of the stars which appeared in them. This did not often happen in European countries. Certainly these countries produced star actors and actresses. Brigitte Bardot, after all, is French. But the biggest names in the European cinema are the names of the people who actually made the films – the directors.

France has produced many films of artistic merit. In the 1920s and 1930s, there were a large number of French film directors, among them René Clair and Jean Renoir, who treated serious subjects seriously and with imagination.

During the Second World War, many of these directors left France. But they returned after the war and new directors joined them. They produced a steady flow of good films, and younger French directors still continue to do so.

At the beginning of the 1920s, some of the most famous films in the world were being made in Germany. As in France, the directors were more famous than the actors and actresses. Fritz Lang, Friedrich Wilhelm Murnau, Robert Wiene and Paul Leni all made remarkable films which were seen all over the world. Mostly they were films of horror and madness.

These films were unusual because they were made entirely in the studios. The cameras were held by machines which allowed them to move and view each scene from new and unusual angles. The backgrounds to the films were specially made by designers who did not feel that it was important to show reality. These German films had a strange atmosphere and a style of their own.

These films were made with great care and they were very expensive. But in the early 1920s, German films earned a lot of money outside Germany. The German studios at Neubabelsberg were the biggest in the world and German directors were able to build whole cities and forests inside them. German directors and cameramen could show things in their films in a more remarkable way than anyone else.

But Hollywood had more money than Germany, and so Hollywood attracted the German directors and cameramen to America. They left Germany and brought their skills to Hollywood. German films slowly became less and less exciting. Finally, the Nazis came to power and good films from Germany became rare.

As the brilliant German directors began to leave Neubabelsberg for Hollywood, the great period of the Russian cinema began. Once again it was the film directors who became famous – Dovzhenko, Pudovkin and, greatest of all, Sergei Eisenstein.

Most of the great German films had been about what went on inside the minds of people. Some of the stories happened in the distant past. And those that happened in the present often showed the effect of society upon the people in it.

The Russian films were quite the opposite. They told of the effect of the individual and of masses of people on society. When they went back into the past, they showed events that had taken place no more than twenty-five years before.

At the time when the Germans had the largest and best equipped film studios in the world, Russian directors were making newsreels in a damp cellar. If the Germans wanted a city scene, they built it specially in the Neubabelsberg studios. The Russians had to go out into their real city streets to make a film. And they had to wait until they could get rolls of film to shoot with.

The wealthy German directors were not happy with the society they lived in. They showed the distant past, horror, individual misery, and madness in their films. The Russian directors were poor, but happy with their society. They showed life around them, full of hope and achievement.

The Russian Revolution had taken place in 1917. It had been followed by a civil war, a war inside Russia itself between the Communists on the one side and the Czarists and Liberals on the other. When the Communists won they had practically no film, no equipment and their film studios were in ruins. Their leader, Lenin, had said: 'Of all the arts, the cinema is the most important to us.'

So Russian film-makers began to build a new Russian film industry. Its aim was to show the Russian people what had happened in the Revolution and how the new Russia was being built.

In many Russian films it was the people who were the heroes. This was often the case in the films of Sergei Eisenstein. Eisenstein made the most famous film of the early Russian cinema, *Battleship Potemkin*. The most famous part of this film is known as the 'Odessa Steps Sequence'.

The action of the film takes place in 1905, at the time of an uprising throughout Russia against the Czar, Nicholas. At Odessa, the sailors on the battleship *Potemkin* take command of the ship from their officers. A crowd comes to watch and cheer them. Many of the people in the crowd are standing on a flight of steps which lead down to the harbour. Cossack soldiers are sent to break up the crowd. The Cossacks walk slowly down the steps, firing on the crowd as they go. Hundreds of people are killed, including women and children. It was a horrifying event and Eisenstein shows the full horror of it on the screen.

Eisenstein shows us the crowd. But he also shows us some of the individual people in the crowd and what happens to them. He keeps moving from the crowd to the individuals and to the Cossacks. We see a baby killed in its mother's arms. The mother does not run away, but

The famous 'Odessa Steps' scene from *Battleship Potemkin* directed by Sergei Eisenstein in 1925 (Sovexport).

walks up the steps towards the Cossack guns.

The horror of the situation is shown with great force, and it is made more forceful by the way in which Eisenstein uses time. Eisenstein moves rapidly from the Cossacks to the crowd and to the individuals. The whole movement of the Cossacks down the Odessa steps takes longer on the screen than it could do in reality.

The Communist government decided what kind of films should be made in Russia. As the years went by, the great Russian film directors found it more and more difficult to work happily with the government. And although Russia still produced great films, like Eisenstein's *Ivan the Terrible*, the number of them became fewer and fewer.

NINE

HOW A FILM IS MADE: THE PRODUCER

In the making of any film, there are two very important people: the producer and the director. Sometimes the same man has been producer and director. And so perhaps we should say that there are two very important jobs: the producer's job, and the director's job. The producer's job starts first, and it also finishes last.

The job of the producer is to gather together the money to make a film. And when the film has been made he has to make sure that it is seen by audiences and that the money is repaid.

The producer's first job is to find a story which will make a good film. Sometimes this may be the story of a novel. In this case, he must buy the rights to make a film of the novel.

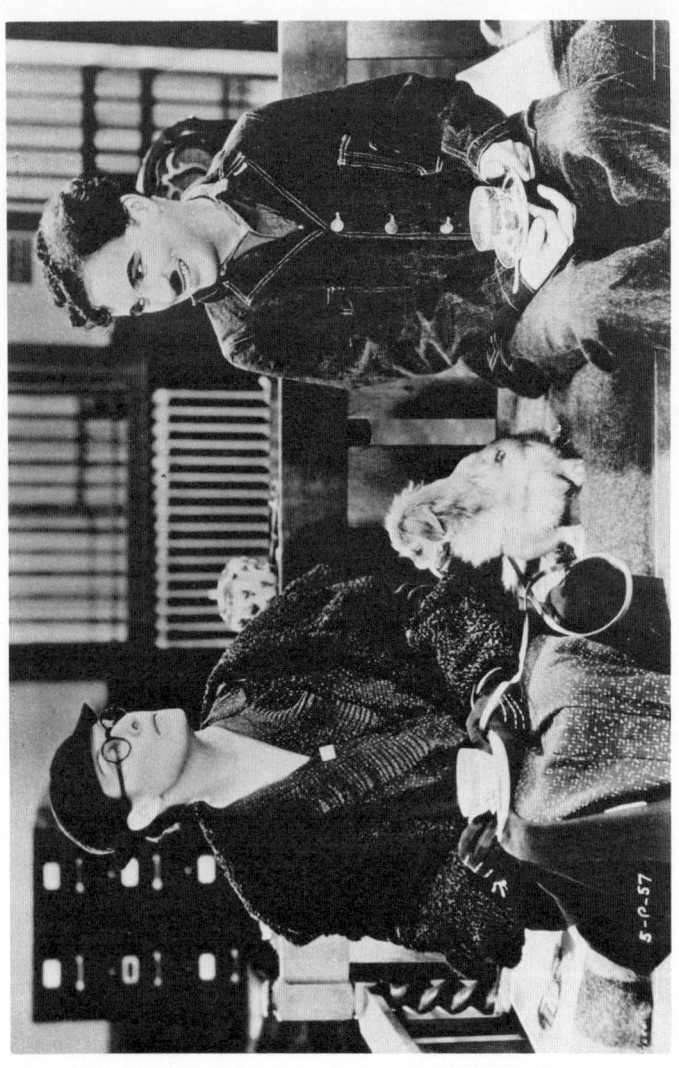

Charlie Chaplin in his film *Modern Times* which he produced, directed and starred in (Paramount Pictures, 1936).

Then the producer has to find a script writer, a director and the actors. And he has to decide how much money the film will cost to make. This money is called the film's budget. If the producer finds a good story, a successful director and famous film stars, then he can give the film a big budget. Sometimes he has money of his own, but usually he must find other people to give money to make the film. These people, who are called backers, hope to receive far more money than they gave. If the film is a success, they do. But if the film is a complete failure, the backers may lose all the money they gave.

The producer must also interest a distributor in his film. The distributor rents the film out to the exhibitors, another name for the cinema-owners. If a good distributor is not found, the film will not reach enough cinemas. Then there will be no chance of the film earning enough money to give its producer and backers a profit.

The producer's next job is to get the public interested in the film. He must get newspapers and magazines to print stories about the film and to show pictures of it being made. He might even make a short film which shows the making of the film. Then he will persuade a television company to show it on television, just before the film appears in the cinemas.

Meanwhile, the producer and director look carefully at the shooting script. This is the complete story of the film, worked out scene by scene and in detail. They decide which scenes of the film have to be shot in the studio and which must be shot outside. Then they can decide how long it will take to make the film.

When the director has made the film for the producer, the producer hands it over to the distributor who puts it into the cinemas.

And so the film is shown. The public decides whether or not it is a success by going to see it or by staying away.

Finally the producer receives the money that the film

earns, and is able to pay his backers. If he can pay them more money than they put into the film, they will think he is a good producer. Perhaps they will then put more money into his next film.

TEN

HOW A FILM IS MADE: THE DIRECTOR

A film belongs to its producer. He has paid for it and it is given to him when it is made. But it is the director who makes the film. When the director has enough freedom, the film says what the director wants it to say. With the greatest films, the director has almost always had this freedom.

There are three people who work closely with a director in the different stages of making a film. They are the script writer, the cameraman and the editor. The director must be able to work well with all three of them if the film is to be really good.

A number of directors have written their films themselves. Griffith did, and so did Eisenstein and Orson Welles. In his later films, Charles Chaplin was producer, director, writer, star, and he even wrote the music. But it is most unusual for one man to do so much work.

Most directors make films from other people's scripts. The director and the writer must both be enthusiastic about the story and understand what the other wants to say. Each of them must have a clear idea of what the film is going to look like before they start filming. When the film is finished, the writer can see his ideas on the screen. And the director should feel that everything looks and sounds the way he wants it.

Although the producer finds the actors, a good producer will discuss his choice with the director. Or the producer will find actors that his director knows and likes. It is part of the director's job to make sure that his actors move and speak in the way that he wants.

Before the first scene of the film is shot, the director plans how the scene will look with his art director. It is the art director's job to build and decorate each scene. Every detail of a scene must be discussed before the art director starts to build it.

The director also discusses each scene with his lighting cameraman. He is the man on whom the whole visual atmosphere of the film depends. A director will often ask for a particular lighting cameraman by name, one that he knows and trusts. Griffith always worked with Billy Bitzer, Eisenstein with Edouard Tissé and Alfred Hitchcock mostly with Robert Burks.

The place in the film studio where the scene is acted is called the set. Before the acting can begin, the lighting cameraman has to light the set. He knows exactly where the actors will stand. He knows how many cameras he is going to use and how the cameras are going to move. If the director wants shadows, the lighting cameraman has to make sure that they are in the right places. The sound engineer works with him. He has to put microphones where they will pick up the actors' voices best. But the microphones must never be seen in the picture the camera takes.

Work starts very early every day and finishes late. There are a great many people working on the set and there are a great many things that can go wrong. There is the director with his assistants, the cameraman and his assistants, the sound engineer and his assistants. And there has to be someone who makes sure that the actors look the same from scene to scene in the completed film.

Sidney Lumet directing Richard Widmark in a scene from *Murder on the Orient Express* with Anthony Perkins in the background (EMI Film Distributors).

Opposite: Albert Finney being 'made-up' for his part as Hercule Poirot in *Murder on the Orient Express* (EMI Film Distributors).

When the film is being made, the scenes are not shot in order. For example, in the first week of shooting, there may be a shot of an actor walking down a street. The following week a scene with the same actor in a room may be shot in the studio. At the end of the scene, the actor leaves the room and, in the completed film, he is seen walking down the street. Clearly, the actor must be wearing exactly the same clothes as before – even his tie must be tied in the same way. The job of getting these things right is called continuity, and the person who does it is called a continuity girl.

There is a famous continuity mistake where a man goes up to a door and opens it. In the next shot he is shown inside the room. And he is wearing a different jacket.

After a long day's work on the set, the film that has been shot is developed and printed during the night. Next

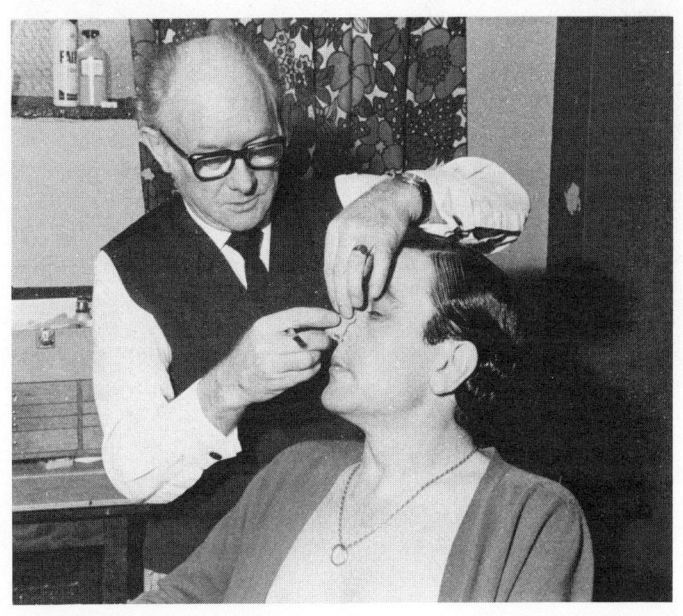

After many hours with the make-up artist, Albert Finney as Hercule Poirot in *Murder on the Orient Express* (EMI Film Distributors).

morning the director looks at it. He will probably have had several copies, or takes, made of the same shot. Some will be impossible to use in the film because something went wrong with them. Perhaps the actor forgot his words, or the sound was not quite right, or the camera moved too fast or too slow. Of all the film shot the day before, the director might only want to use two or three minutes in the completed film.

In the end, all the shooting is finished and the director can start the final stage of making the film. This is called editing. Here the hundreds of pieces of film are cut up and stuck together in the right order. This is done by the editor. Like the script writer and the cameraman, the editor must also work closely with the director. He must understand clearly what the director wants. A good editor can make a good film better. Sometimes he can make a dull film interesting. D. W. Griffith has always been admired for the way in which he used editing in his films. But perhaps the most famous piece of editing of all time is the 'Odessa Steps Sequence' in Eisenstein's *Battleship Potemkin*.

Griffith and Eisenstein were editing silent, black and white film. A modern editor has a more complicated job. He works with colour and sound too.

Much of the excitement in a film is created at the editing stage. The editor and the director decide how quickly one shot must follow the next. If the action in a film goes too slowly, the audience can become bored by it. But if the action goes too quickly, the audience becomes confused.

Once the film is edited, the music can be written. Music can be extremely useful to a film director, if he uses it carefully. It is used mainly to produce the kind of emotion in the audience that the director wants. The music for a film is written with care, and the editor fits it into all the right places.

The last job that the director must do is called dubbing.

The man he works with is called the dubbing mixer. The dubbing mixer takes all the different tracks of sound, and dubs or joins them together onto one single track.

When this is done, the director sends the film to the processing laboratory. There the first print or showprint is made and the film is completed.

A film director once said that directing a film is the easiest job in the world. Everyone else, he said, does your work for you.

This is partly true. We have seen that the director works with other people all the time. But the director must know from the beginning what he wants the film to look like. And he must make sure that everyone understands what he wants. Sometimes that is not the easiest thing in the world.

ELEVEN

FILM TYPES: EPIC AND COMIC

So far we have talked about the story of Hollywood and some of the European film industries. We have seen how a modern film is made. But we have not looked very closely at the films themselves.

Millions of films have been made and clearly we cannot look at many if we look at them one by one. But we can consider various types of films. In this chapter, we shall look at two of the most popular types, the epic and the comic.

The Epic

To most people, an epic film is one that is at least two

hours long. It must have a lot of actors and cost a lot of money to make. There must also be at least one battle in it.

A film critic will say that an epic tells a story of an historical event and of the people who took part in it. And so, to a film critic, *Battleship Potemkin* is an epic even though it is not a long film and did not cost a very great deal to make.

The first epics were made in Italy and France. It was the success of Guazzoni's *Quo Vadis?* and Pastrone's *Cabiria* in the United States that prepared American audiences for Griffith's *The Birth of a Nation* and *Intolerance*, both epic films.

Griffith's two epics showed the world that film could be a form of art. But epic films have not often reached the level of art. Mostly, epic films have tried to impress their audiences with their size. They have all had large budgets – most of them have cost several million dollars. They have had huge numbers of actors in them. Their stories have been about great historical characters like Napoleon, or Cleopatra. Other epics have had stories about great historical events like the revolt of the slaves in ancient Rome or the American Civil War.

There have also been epic films which tell stories from the Bible. The earliest of these was *The Passion of Our Lord Jesus Christ*, which Ferdinand Zecca made in France between 1902 and 1905. It lasted for about half an hour, which was a very long time in the early 1900s. And in the 1960s, John Huston made a very long epic called, simply, *The Bible*. Some of the most famous epics have had stories set in Biblical times, like *Ben Hur* and *The Robe*.

The size of epic films makes people remember them. People who went to the cinema in the 1920s still remember Fred Niblo's *Ben Hur* with Ramon Novarro. The film was released in 1927, but work had begun on it before 1923. Its size was amazing. 150,000 people worked on it

The famous chariot-race in *Ben Hur* directed by Fred Niblo (MGM, 1927). [From the MGM release 'BEN HUR' © 1927 Metro-Goldwyn-Mayer Distributing Corporation. Copyright renewed 1955 by Loew's Incorporated.]

and it cost four million dollars to make. A hundred Roman warships were specially built for a naval battle. Every detail of the six thousand Roman uniforms was accurate. A copy of the Roman circus arena at Antioch was built near Culver City in the USA and, again, every detail was correct.

In spite of size, cost and accuracy of details, it is still difficult for words and story to come alive in an epic. Perhaps this is why so few epics have been works of art. But even the worst epic produces a feeling of wonder at the cost of the thing. *The Alamo*, an epic about a battle between Americans and Mexicans, cost more to make than the battle cost to fight.

The Comic Film

There is a period in the history of the cinema which is sometimes called 'The Age of Comedy'. This was from about 1910 to 1925 in America.

During this time, Griffith was making his famous epics in the Mamaronek studios in California. Meanwhile, his partner in the Triangle Company, Mack Sennett, was making a huge number of short comedy films in his Keystone studios.

Griffith's films were planned down to the last detail. Sennett's films seldom had a proper script. He made them in a very short time, and in its first year the studios made about three films a week. The films were very fast and full of movement. Cups and plates were broken, walls were knocked down, custard pies were thrown in people's faces. Sennett believed that policemen could be very funny and he made a large number of films with his famous Keystone Kops. These were all comic chases in which the cars of his Kops, or policemen, rushed around at great speed and often broke into pieces.

After a time Sennett's films were more carefully prepared. He himself worked out the stories. Then he gave them to a group of writers who put in as many jokes as they could think of. Even so, scripts were often changed during shooting.

Sennett's greatest success was in finding comic actors. Almost all the comedians of the time worked at Keystone. Among them was the most famous film comic in the world, Charlie Chaplin.

It was at Keystone that Chaplin first worked in films. He made thirty-five films there altogether, including *Tillie's Punctured Romance*, the first feature-length American comedy. In *The Kid Auto Races at Venice*, Chaplin wore for the first time the tramp costume in which he became famous.

Chaplin left Keystone and moved from company to company, making more and more money as he became more famous. His tramp character became more complicated. He became sad at times, as well as funny. He became the little man fighting the big, hard world.

Chaplin's films became longer and also took more time and money to make. *The Gold Rush*, possibly his best film, cost a million dollars. In this film, Chaplin's little tramp character is searching for gold in Alaska. There is snow everywhere and the tramp is pushed into it most of the time. He finds himself in a small wooden cabin, miles away from anywhere, and with no food. And so he cooks one of his boots and shares it with a huge gold-miner. The little tramp eats his piece of boot politely and carefully. This scene shows Chaplin's humour at its most perfect. It is both sad and extremely funny at the same time.

Another well-known comedian who was popular at the same time was Buster Keaton. In Keaton's films, his face never moved. He never smiled or looked afraid. But the rest of his body moved with the greatest of energy. He seemed as if he never knew what he was doing. His finest film was *The General* which he made in 1926.

When sound came to the cinema, most of the comedians of 'The Age of Comedy' were unable to make the change. Chaplin brought out the silent film, *City Lights*, four years after *The Jazz Singer* had made sound popular. And even *Modern Times*, which came out five years later, in 1936, used very little speech.

Mack Sennett was not able to work well in sound. But his great rival as a producer of comedies, Hal Roach, was more fortunate. He had in his studios two comedians who succeeded in sound where so many others failed. They were Stan Laurel and Oliver Hardy.

Laurel and Hardy's success came with sound. But what they did on the screen was always more funny than what they said. In their films they always tried to do the right thing and it always went wrong. They then tried to put it right and everything went wrong. One accident followed another, and this sometimes led to an entire house being destroyed.

The Marx Brothers came from the theatre in 1929 to make a film called *The Cocoanuts* and went on to make a number of films during the 1930s and 1940s. Trying to do good, Laurel and Hardy broke up the world around them. The Marx Brothers made trouble on purpose. There were three of them: Groucho, Chico and Harpo. In their early films, a fourth brother, Zeppo, joined them. The humour of Groucho and Chico was mainly in the words they spoke. But Harpo did not speak at all. He was a silent comedian in a world of sound. Most of their films were spoilt by having dull and unimaginative stories. In only two or three of their films did the story and their humour work together.

The very best of film comedy has almost always been what was shown on the screen, rather than what was said. Jacques Tati, the great modern French comedian, has made films since the 1950s which were funnier to look at than to listen to. As with Laurel and Hardy, the world around Jacques Tati goes wrong in spite of his efforts to do the right thing. In his fourth film, *Traffic*, he uses very few words and the audience can hardly hear them at all.

People still enjoy the old silent comedies, the films of 'The Age of Comedy'. They are the only films from the silent days in which we do not notice that sound is missing.

TWELVE

FILM TYPES: WESTERNS, GANGSTERS AND MUSICALS

The Western

Western films take place in the American West. The stories usually take place between the 1820s and 1880s, although *Lonely Are the Brave* was a Western too. And that refers to events in the early 1960s.

The American West of the 19th century was an unpleasant place. Most people carried guns, and life in the West was full of fighting and sudden death. Life was changing quickly and the changes caused trouble.

In the early days of the cinema, the West of the Westerns still existed in many places. It was wild and violent. But to people living in the East of the United States, the West was still a place of adventure and excitement. And it was, of course, people living in the East who made these early films.

Edwin Porter's film, *The Great Train Robbery*, was a Western. But Porter's film was not the first Western. Western life and Western stories were so popular that they were used in the very first films ever made.

Later, when the American cinema industry moved to Hollywood, the third of the Triangle Company studios, Thomas Ince's Inceville, made Westerns. The hero of Ince's films was William S. Hart and the stories were usually about a bad man who became good at the end of the story.

In the 1920s new Western heroes, like Tom Mix, became popular. They rode around the West on their horses doing good. They did not drink. When they fought, they fought with their fists. When sound came, these good cowboys became singing cowboys too. They were always playing guitars. This kind of cowboy, who had never existed in the real West, remained popular up to the 1950s. Roy Rogers was one of the last of the type. In his films he never smoked, never drank alcohol, never kissed or fell in love with a woman. He loved only his horse.

These actors appeared in popular Westerns, but not in good Westerns.

The first of the famous Western films was *The Covered Wagon*. It was an epic and told the story of a group of people travelling to California in 1849. They travelled in covered wagons, the only way for people to carry their belongings from East to West. The journey was extremely difficult. The story of the journey and the beautiful scenery made the film exciting and interesting to look at. *The Covered Wagon* was made in 1923. The following year another great Western was made. It was called *The Iron Horse* and its director was John Ford. It told the story of how the railway was first built from the East to California.

In 1939, John Ford made the most famous Western of all. The title of the film was *Stagecoach*. It told the story of passengers on a journey by stagecoach. They are attacked by Indians and the film ends with a magnificent gunfight. As in *The Covered Wagon*, the harsh and

Stagecoach directed by John Ford in 1939 (Anthony Morris [London] Ltd).

beautiful scenery of the West made *Stagecoach* a very attractive film to look at.

The Hollywood studios made a great many Westerns. And a great many people went to the cinema to see them. These audiences felt they knew the West well. They knew what the country looked like and how the people lived there. There were the cowboys, who looked after the huge herds of cattle and lived on farms called ranches. There were the Indians, who had lived on the land before the white men came. From time to time, the Indians fought the white men who were taking more and more of their land. There was the US cavalry, soldiers on horses, who fought the Indians. In many films, the cavalry arrived just in time to stop the Indians killing groups of white men.

Later, there was another reason for fighting. More people came to the West. They made small farms in the great open spaces. When the small farmers came and fenced in the land, the ranch owners' cattle could not wander freely. This caused a great deal of trouble. George Stevens' famous Western, *Shane*, and the Western musical, *Oklahoma!*, both use this situation as a background to their stories.

In the towns of the West, the sheriffs tried to keep law and order. *High Noon*, a famous Western made in 1952 by Fred Zinnemann, tells the story of a sheriff. He is left by the people of his town to fight a group of outlaws on his own.

Outlaws often appeared in Westerns. They robbed banks, stagecoaches and trains. There was always plenty of empty land where they could hide.

Because the audiences knew the people and the background of the West, it was possible to tell all kinds of stories using a Western background. In the 1960s it became too expensive to make Westerns in America. Hollywood began to make them in Spain and Italy. And the Italians made their own Westerns.

Why is the Western so popular? In the West, people had to rule themselves. They had to decide what was right and what was wrong. It was easy to see who was a good man and who was a bad man. A man who shoots another man in the back is bad. We can see that at once. It was easy to make stories like this into popular films.

People in the West had to work hard and strong men were often more successful than thinking men. There was not a lot of time for thinking. Speed with a gun was more important. It was easier to make a film about the West than about a place where ideas were more complicated.

The Gangster Film

The outlaws of the West were only a part of Western films. But the Chicago gangsters of the 1920s, who were outlaws too, have films all to themselves.

In 1920, the United States passed a law which made the sale of alcoholic drinks illegal throughout the country. Many people did not like the law and small criminals became wealthy by selling alcohol illegally.

The criminals came together in gangs, and the gangs in Chicago and New York were very strong. The strongest gangs took over other gangs and killed their leaders.

Throughout the middle and the late 1920s, American newspapers were full of stories about the gangsters, especially about Al Capone of Chicago and Arnold Rothstein of New York.

In 1927, Josef von Sternberg made a film called *Underworld*. It was the first film to put the newspaper stories onto the screen. *Underworld* was written by Ben Hecht, who had been a newspaper reporter. Ben Hecht went on to write some of the best gangster films. In 1931, fifty gangster films were made. Josef von Sternberg had made *Underworld* for the Paramount studios, but it was the Warner Brothers studios which made the best gangster films.

By the time Hollywood was telling their stories, most of the gangsters were either dead or in prison. But the streets of the cities where they had lived were still there. Actors like Paul Muni, Edward G. Robinson, James Cagney and George Raft made the stories fast and exciting.

The stories showed the real lives of the gangsters, and the gangsters were the main characters in the films. At first, the Hay's Office objected to them. But the Hay's Office made no problems if the police won in the end.

The true gangster films had been stories of real events as they happened. Although many gangster films were made after 1933, they were no longer about the life of their own time. They were about history.

The Musical

In the 1930s, the Warner Brothers studios were famous for their gangster films. And they were also famous for their musicals. They had made the first sound film, *The Jazz Singer*, and that had been a musical. A musical tells its story with songs and, very often, dances too.

When the sound came to the cinema in the late 1920s, musicals were very popular in the New York theatres. Hollywood used actors from the theatre for its new sound films. It believed that the things that were popular in the theatre would be popular in films. The musicals certainly were.

Warner Brothers employed Busby Berkeley, a dance director from New York, for many of their musicals. Busby Berkeley soon learnt to show song and dance in films in a new and exciting way. In films like *42nd Street*, *Footlight Parade* and *The Gold Diggers of '33*, he used large numbers of dancers to make complicated patterns on the screen. The stories of the films he worked on often

James Cagney in the 'gangster film', *The Roaring Twenties* (United Artists, 1939).

One of the scenes from the musical, *The Gold Diggers of '33* staged by **Busby Berkeley** (United Artists).

stopped completely while his complicated songs and dances were shown.

The RKO studios had two very famous dancers for their musicals. They were Fred Astaire and Ginger Rogers. In their films, the songs and dances were always more a part of the story than in Busby Berkeley's films. The dances were clever and elegant. They can be seen at their best in films like *Top Hat* and *Swing Time*.

Hollywood produced a great many musicals during the 1930s and the 1940s. In the 1940s the biggest stars were Frank Sinatra and Gene Kelly in films like *On the Town* and *Anchors Aweigh*. And there was Judy Garland in *The Wizard of Oz*, *Babes in Arms* and *Meet Me in St Louis*.

Most of the musicals of the 1930s and the 1940s were specially written for the cinema. In the 1950s and 1960s more and more theatre musicals were filmed.

The musicals were meant to look attractive and many took place in attractive backgrounds.

Oklahoma!, *South Pacific*, *The King and I* and other musicals written by Richard Rodgers and Oscar Hammerstein had been successful in the theatre and were also successful in the cinemas in the 1950s.

Most of the musicals of the 1960s, taken from the theatre, were very expensive to make. Lerner and Loewe's *My Fair Lady* was a great success in the New York theatre. Five and a half million dollars were paid for the rights to make a film of it. The final cost of the film was enormous, but it earned more money than it had cost.

Other expensive musicals of the 1960s lost money, like *Doctor Dolittle*, which had cost twenty-eight million dollars to make and distribute.

But the most successful musical and, for its time, the most successful film ever, was Rodgers and Hammerstein's *The Sound of Music* with Julie Andrews. Film critics did not like it at all, but the public loved it.

THIRTEEN

ANIMATION AND SPECIAL EFFECTS

Long before the Lumières made their first camera and projector, there were machines which showed movement. They did not use film. Instead they used drawings. These machines showed very simple movements: a man running, a man kicking a ball, a bird flying. When audiences could see films, they forgot the animated or moving drawings of earlier years.

But drawings could be put onto film and made to move. It was slow and difficult work; each second of movement needed twenty-four different drawings. The advantage of drawings is that they do not need to look real. Tricks had made the films of Georges Méliès popular. Even more amazing tricks could be shown in animated films. Large numbers of short animated films were made by many people in the late 1900s and 1910s. Most of them used these amazing tricks.

But it was Walt Disney who made animated films really popular. In the 1920s, Disney had been making animated films called *Alice in Cartoonland* and *Oswald the Rabbit* with some success. Then he produced one of the most famous film characters of all time: Mickey Mouse. The third Mickey Mouse film, *Steamboat Willie*, came out in 1928, one year after *The Jazz Singer*. *Steamboat Willie* was the first animated film to have speech and music. Its success was immediate. In 1932, Disney produced *Flowers and Trees*, the first film in the new three-colour Technicolor process.

Disney was an excellent businessman. He made his animated films as cheaply and quickly as possible. This was most important when fourteen thousand separate drawings were needed to make a ten-minute film. Large numbers of people worked for Disney and each one had his own special job.

Disney soon gave Mickey Mouse a number of other animal friends. The first was a girl mouse, called Minnie. Then came Pluto, a foolish dog, and Donald Duck.

In 1937, Disney made *Snow White and the Seven Dwarfs*. It was a full-length feature film. It was another very successful film, and more feature-length animated films followed.

Disney was the most successful maker of animated films. But once he had made the animated film popular, other Hollywood studios began to make animated films too. The most successful of these were the *Popeye the Sailor* films, which Max Fleischer made for Paramount.

The Popeye films were much rougher than the Mickey Mouse ones. The drawings had less detail and the stories were full of violence.

Popeye had an enemy, called Bluto. Bluto always started a fight, often by taking away Popeye's girlfriend, Olive Oyl. In every fight, Popeye was badly beaten at the beginning. Then he ate a tin of spinach which gave him great strength. After that, he always won the fight.

Max Fleischer used the trick possibilities of animated film far more than Disney. Popeye's fists turned into rushing railway engines. He could change himself into a gun and shoot himself at Bluto. And Bluto was stretched, squashed and knocked right off the earth into space.

Violence has appeared in a large number of animated films since the late 1930s. Bugs Bunny, a rabbit, uses speed and intelligence to beat a small, round-faced hunter who is always chasing him with a gun. Sylvester, the cat, is always beaten when he tries to catch the bird, Tweetie Pie. Tom and Jerry, a cat and a mouse, were first made by William Hanna and Joseph Barbera for MGM. Tom, the

Mickey Mouse as the ringmaster and Pluto the dog as the lion in the cartoon film, *Mickey's Circus* (© Walt Disney Productions).

cat, is always in trouble. He is squashed flat, loses his skin and is frozen into blocks of ice.

There are also a large number of serious animated films. Many of them are very unusual. For example, sometimes they show nothing more than a moving dot or line. The Zagreb Film Studio of Yugoslavia and the National Film Board of Canada have made many films of this kind, in which animated film becomes an art.

In the last twenty years, animated films have been made for television rather than for the cinema. Studios now make them much less carefully than Disney did. Instead of using twenty-four pictures a second they can now use as few as four. The movements in these films are very sudden and unreal, but this does not trouble the audiences. Also, the pictures in an animated film can now be made by computer. Computers are expensive but they can do a lot of work in a short time. A large number of animated films have to be produced to keep the computer busy. The result is that many of these films are dull and unimaginative.

Special Effects

When a film has to show something that seems real but is not real, its director will often use special effects.

Special effects is another name for trick photography. It has always been popular in films. The first film shown to the public in one of Edison's kinetoscopes used special effects. It showed an axe cutting off the head of Mary, Queen of Scots.

Later, Méliès used special effects in almost all of his films. He showed a man's head on a table in his film *The Inflatable Head*. The head is blown up bigger and bigger like a balloon.

A great many films use special effects in small ways. A character in a Western is shot with an Indian's arrow. We see the arrow sticking into him but we know that this is not real. It is a special effect.

There are certain kinds of films that use a great many special effects. There are the fantasy films. For example, in *The Cabinet of Dr Caligari*, all the scenery looks unreal and it is only at the end of the film that we understand why. It was the scenery of a madman's nightmare.

Another kind of film that uses special effects is the horror film. Horror films are full of ghosts and monsters. It is easy to show a ghost on the screen. Anybody who has accidentally used the same piece of film in a camera twice knows how easy it is. One picture appears like a ghost on top of the other picture. This is called double exposure. In films, the picture of the actor who plays the ghost is added to the picture of the scene he is meant to appear in. The result is like double exposure and the technique is called superimposition.

Horror films try to make the audience feel afraid, and ghosts are often frightening. But they can easily be funny too, and have been used in comedies like *The Canterville Ghost* and *The Ghost Goes West*.

Monsters usually need better special effects than ghosts. An example is the story of Dr Jekyll and Mr Hyde, which has been made into at least five films. In the story, the good and handsome Dr Jekyll changes into the evil monster, Mr Hyde. In the films, the change is often made with special effects. The best of these was in Rouben Mamoulian's film of the story in 1932. Dr Jekyll's face is seen on the screen all the time as he changes into the monstrous Mr Hyde. Mamoulian did this simply by changing the lights in the studio.

Many of the cinema's favourite monsters have hardly needed special effects at all. Frankenstein's monster, so often acted by Boris Karloff and Bela Lugosi, only needed make-up.

Other monsters have been too large or too small for make-up alone. One of these was the most famous monster of all. His name was King Kong and he appeared first in a film made in 1932. King Kong was a giant gorilla. The film, *King Kong*, used a great many special effects and some were very good, using models and superimposition. But the monster gorilla keeps changing his size, and this was an accident. All the same, the film was very popular. And horror films are still popular. The British film company, Hammer Films, became successful through their horror films.

And then there are the scientific horror and adventure films. Films like *Destination Moon*, *The Conquest of Space* and *2001* showed future space travel and used small models of rocket ships and space stations very

The giant gorilla, King Kong with Fay Wray in the film, *King Kong* made in 1932.

cleverly.

Science also made monsters. In a film called *Them*, atomic radiation produced giant ants. Huge models and superimposition were used and the giant ants were completely believable.

In epic films many big, spectacular scenes use special effects. If a city must burn to the ground, a model must be used. If there is a sea battle it is cheaper to sink model ships than real ones. To make the small splashes of water look real, the film is shown in slow motion.

These spectacular effects have now become so technically perfect that huge films like *Earthquake* and *Towering Inferno* depend entirely on successful special effects.

FOURTEEN

THE CINEMA IN BRITAIN

The British film industry has always had difficulties. In the early years of the cinema, British film-makers did a great deal of interesting and useful work. They discovered many of the editing techniques that Griffith later used. The early British film-makers were practical scientists. They were more interested in their machinery than in their stories. There were no film-makers as great as Griffiths or Méliès in Britain.

At the end of 1913, a young English comedian took a job with Mack Sennett in California. The comedian was Charlie Chaplin. And so Charlie Chaplin was lost to the British film industry.

After the First World War, Hollywood's films were much better than films made in Britain. In 1927, the British government passed a law to make British cinemas show British films. The law was meant to help the British film industry, but it only made things worse. A certain number of British films had to be shown in British cinemas every year. The audience, however, did not worry if the British films were good or bad. They wanted to see the Hollywood films that were in the same programme. And so the British films were made as cheaply as possible, and they were bad.

One reason for Hollywood's success was that the American film industry had its own writers, directors and actors. They did not come from the theatre because Hollywood was a long way from New York, where the biggest American theatres were. But the British studios were either in or near London, and so they used theatrical writers and actors for their films.

In 1929, John Grierson started making documentary films in Britain. Grierson used real life for his stories and real people for his actors. The documentary film-makers made short films. The money to make them came from the British government.

Alexander Korda's film, *The Private Life of Henry VIII*, was the first British film to reach a large number of American cinemas. It made a great deal of money.

The British film industry was delighted. It tried to make other films to sell in America, but it failed. In Korda's film, Henry VIII was played by an English actor, Charles Laughton, who had acted in Hollywood. It was partly because Laughton was already known in America that *The Private Life of Henry VIII* was successful there. The British studios then used American actors and American and French directors in very expensive films. But none of these films were very successful in America, and they lost money.

In the Second World War, the British documentary and feature film-makers came together to make films about Britain at war. The mixture of documentary and story was good. From the documentary film-makers came a feeling for the truth. From the feature film-makers came an understanding of working in studios and of telling a story in an exciting way.

After the war, the British film industry had actors and directors who were able to make good films. The directors, Carol Reed and David Lean, made films of international importance. David Lean's *Brief Encounter*, made in 1945, tells a very simple story about two people who fall in love. The woman has a husband and a family, the man has a wife and family. Finally they decide to remain with their own families. It is not a dramatic or an exciting story. The film was successful because it kept its audience interested in the two people all the time. The following year, David Lean made *Great Expectations*, one of the best films to be made from a Dickens novel.

Carol Reed's *Odd Man Out*, which was made in 1947, was very dramatic. James Mason, as Johnny MacQueen, is wounded and is bleeding to death. He wanders through the streets of Belfast, trying to find somewhere to hide. As well as being an exciting story, *Odd Man Out* gives a strong feeling of the city of Belfast.

Two years later, in *The Third Man*, Carol Reed gave a powerful picture of another city, Vienna. An American writer arrives in Vienna, looking for his friend, Harry Lime. He is told that Harry Lime has been killed, and tries to find out what happened. He discovers that Harry Lime is a criminal and that he is still alive. The film ends with a chase, and finally Harry Lime is really killed. The city of Vienna seems full of wet streets, old ruined buildings and black shadows.

In the 1940s and early 1950s, there were also a large number of good British comedy films. Many of these were made in the Ealing Studios of Sir Michael Balcon. *Kind Hearts and Coronets*, made in 1949 by Robert Hamer, was very different from other comedy films of

A scene from David Lean's film made in 1946, *Great Expectations* (by courtesy of Rank Organisation Ltd).

the time. The main character is a young man who murders eight of his relations. Crime was often used for humour in later Ealing comedies. In *The Lavender Hill Mob*, in 1951, a bank clerk steals three million pounds. In *The Ladykillers*, several robbers try to kill an old lady and get killed themselves.

The Ealing comedies were successful and they were not expensive to make. Sir Michael Balcon made them for British cinemas. The British cinemas showed them and they made a profit. When American cinemas also showed them, then they made a big profit.

But the head of another British studio, J. Arthur Rank, made much more expensive films. They had to do well in America to make a profit. His films were good, but they did not do well in America and he lost a lot of money.

In the middle 1950s, almost all the British studios were in difficulties. Many of the best British directors and actors had gone to work in America. And a large number of the films made in Britain after that were made with American money.

But films were still made, and new kinds of films. In 1958, Jack Clayton made *Room at the Top*. It was the first of a number of films which showed the painful side of ordinary life. Most of the British directors who made these films went to Hollywood to make more successful ones.

In the early 1940s, there were about 4,750 cinemas in Britain. In the early 1960s, there were about 3,000. In the early 1970s, there were only 1,500. Recently, even more cinemas have closed in Britain.

In other European countries, fewer cinemas have closed. Cinemas in Britain have perhaps suffered so badly because British television, particularly in the 1960s, was so good. People in Britain did not need to go out for good entertainment.

Very few films are now made in Britain. But there are

One of the successful British comedies of the 1950s from the Ealing Studios, *The Ladykillers* (EMI Film Distributors).

still a number of very good British film directors. They learnt in the 1950s and 1960s how good films were made. They now work all over the world. But because today so few films are made in Britain, it is difficult for new British directors to learn their job.

FIFTEEN

THE CINEMA AROUND THE WORLD

Many countries have film industries and many of them began between 1896 and 1898. This was because the Lumière brothers decided to send their new machine, the Cinématographe, to so many countries. In 1896, there were Cinématographes in Britain, Austria, Switzerland, Hungary, Yugoslavia, Russia, Sweden, India, Australia and several other countries. In 1897, the Cinématographe reached Japan.

Hollywood made films for the whole world, and each year it made a great many. But there were, and still are, two other countries that make large numbers of films.

One of these is India. When Britain had 4,750 cinemas, India had 1,700. Now Britain has fewer than 1,500 and India has over 5,250. In the early 1970s, India was making over 425 feature films a year. That was more than Hollywood was making in the great days of the middle 1940s. The film stars of the Indian cinema, people like Sivaji Ganesan and M. G. Ramachandran, can attract huge crowds when they appear in public. They are far more important to the people of India than the American film stars are now to the people of America.

In India, the cinema is still the main form of entertainment. Few people have the money to buy television sets, but they can see a film for very little money.

And so India now has the biggest film industry in the world. In the 1950s and early 1960s, the Indian director, Satyajit Ray, made a number of films that were shown throughout the world. The first of these was *Pather Panchali*.

But there are not many good Indian films. Most Indian films follow the same pattern. They have six songs, several dances and many different ways of showing men and women kissing without their lips ever touching.

Before the Second World War, Hollywood was making a very large number of films each year. From 1937 to 1938, India made 200 films and Hollywood made 545. But there was one country at that time, and one alone, which made more films than Hollywood. This was Japan. Later, in 1956, Hollywood made just over 300 films. And Japan made over 500.

The first cinema to show films in Japan was built in 1903. The first film studio was built in 1908. Most early Japanese films were very like the Japanese theatre on the screen. In the Japanese theatre, men played the parts of women. It was not until 1918 that a woman was used to act a woman's part in a Japanese film.

There were three main kinds of stories in Japanese films. These were traditional warrior stories, love stories, and stories about everyday life.

Japan fought a number of successful wars before the Second World War. As the country became stronger, more and more cinemas throughout the Far East began to show Japanese films. This made the Japanese film industry very wealthy. But most Japanese films were made cheaply. Japanese producers did not spend so much on a film as the Hollywood producers did. And so they were able to make more films than the Hollywood producers.

As Japan fought war after war, the military forces became more and more powerful inside the country. Throughout the 1930s, films about war became very popular, and fewer films about everyday life were allowed to be made. Japan's defeat in the Second World War meant that very few films were made at all in the middle 1940s. But the Japanese film industry quickly recovered after the war.

Japan had made many films, but few of them were seen in America and Europe until 1951. In that year, the first prize at the Venice Film Festival was given to a film by the Japanese director, Akira Kurosawa. The film was called *Rashomon*. In the next eighteen years, over 400 Japanese films won prizes at international film festivals. One of the most famous was *The Seven Samurai*. It was made in 1954, and was also by Akira Kurosawa.

In *The Seven Samurai*, a medieval Japanese village is attacked by bandits. The villagers decide to look for fighting men, called samurai, to fight the bandits for them. Seven samurai agree, and go to the village. There are many more bandits than samurai. The samurai build a wall of sharp sticks around the village, fight a number of battles with the bandits and kill several of them. In the end there is a final battle in the rain.

Many Japanese films did not have stories in the same way as the Hollywood films. Stories were not as important to the Japanese and their Far Eastern audiences. But *The Seven Samurai* does have a story. Akira Kurosawa said that he had made the film like a Western. And *The Seven Samurai* does have a story similar to many Westerns. The scenery looks very different from the American West, but the Japanese villagers are like the Western farmers and the samurai are like the Western cowboys. The bandits are like the Western outlaws. In the 1960s, Hollywood made a film called *The Magnificent Seven*. It was a

The Seven Samurai directed by Akira Kurosawa in 1954 (Connoisseur Films Ltd).

Western which took place in Mexico, and its story was almost exactly the same as the story of *The Seven Samurai*.

Japan, India and Hollywood are the homes of the biggest film industries in the world. Next come Britain, France, Germany and Italy. But there are also a large number of other countries that make films. They do not make many films, and few of them are seen by international audiences. The films from these countries that are seen internationally are usually the work of one or two very good directors.

The animated films of the Zagreb studios in Yugoslavia are often seen in other countries. Animated films also come from Czechoslovakia, where they were made by Jiri Trnka. Luis Bunuel is a Spanish film director whose films are seen by international audiences. The films of Ingmar Bergman of Sweden are well known throughout the world.

The Future

The cinema became the greatest entertainment industry in the world because millions of people paid to see films.

But today, in many countries, people prefer to watch television. In countries where a lot of people watch television, fewer films are made. And there are fewer and fewer cinemas to show them. But this does not mean that there will come a time when no films are made and there are no cinemas left.

The cinema did not really become a form of art for almost twenty years. But, since Griffith's *The Birth of a Nation*, the cinema has been a form of art and will continue to be one. Most films have been made for entertainment only. But a number of film directors have always tried to do more than entertain. And their films have been works of art.

In the future, this kind of film will become more and more important. The cinema, which began as entertainment, may perhaps live on as art.

POINTS FOR UNDERSTANDING

CHAPTER 1

1. Where can the earliest pictures in the world be seen?
2. Where does the word 'cinema' come from?
3. What is the name of the most important place in the American film industry?
4. Why was *The Jazz Singer* important?
5. Which film started a revolution in Western pop music?
6. Why was Hollywood called 'the dream factory'?

CHAPTER 2

1. What was important about the camera in the filming of *The Great Train Robbery*?
2. Many machines were used in the early days of filming. Give the names of any three of them.
3. Why was the cinema international from the beginning?
4. Who made the first use of trick photography and what was the name of his most famous film?
5. What was *Film d'Art*?

CHAPTER 3

1. How many actors took part in the making of *The Fall of Troy*?
2. How long did *The Great Train Robbery* last?
3. What were the advantages of California for film companies?
4. Which three companies formed the Triangle Company?
5. Why did Griffith make *Judith of Bethulia* secretly?
6. Why did Biograph not allow close-ups in their films?
7. How long did *Birth of a Nation* run?
8. In 1910, audiences did not know the names of any American film actors. Why?
9. How much was Charlie Chaplin earning in 1917?

CHAPTER 4

1. What sounds did the audiences hear in the early silent films?
2. What were sub-titles for?
3. What is synchronisation and who succeeded in perfecting it?
4. What was the name of Warner Brothers' first big sound film and who was its star?
5. Why did some film stars lose their jobs after 1928?

CHAPTER 5

1. What did Hollywood consider a successful film?
2. Why are the stories of so many films very similar to one another?
3. When was the first colour photograph taken?
4. Why did film audiences not like colour at first?
5. How was colour used in *The Wizard of Oz*?
6. What is the purpose of a documentary film?
7. Who first used the word 'documentary'?
8. About how many documentary films were made in Britain during the war?

CHAPTER 6

1. What advantages did television have over the cinema?
2. Why were more and more films made in colour?
3. Explain the following terms: Cinerama; stereophonic sound; Natural Vision; CinemaScope.
4. What was the first film shown in CinemaScope?
5. Why did every Hollywood studio have to have its own stars?
6. Why did the studios often employ young, unknown actors? And why did they often give them new names?
7. How did Raquel Welch begin her career as a film star?

CHAPTER 7

1. Why did television companies want to buy Hollywood's old films?
2. Why had the star system broken down by the 1960s?
3. What was the Hay's Office?
4. What were 'B' pictures?
5. What happened to the Hollywood film companies in the 1960s and 1970s?

CHAPTER 8

1. Why did Hollywood not make many films of artistic merit?
2. Name one famous film director from:
    (a) France;   (b) Germany;   (c) Russia.
3. What did Lenin say about the cinema?
4. What part of the film *Battleship Potemkin* is best known?

CHAPTER 9

1. In the making of a film, whose job starts first and finishes last?
2. What is a film's budget?
3. Who are the backers?
4. Who decides if a film is successful or not?

CHAPTER 10

1. Who does a film belong to?
2. Who makes a film?
3. What was unusual about some of Chaplin's later films?
4. What is the work of:

    (a) an art director?   (b) a cameraman?
    (c) a sound engineer?   (d) a continuity girl?
    (e) an editor?   (f) a dubbing-mixer?

5. How many minutes of completed film may be produced after one day's work on the set?
6. When is the music for a film written?

CHAPTER 11

1. Name an epic film made by each of the following: (a) Griffith; (b) Huston; (c) Eisenstein; (d) Fred Niblo; (e) Guazzoni.
2. What was strange about the epic film, *The Alamo*?
3. When was the 'Age of Comedy'?
4. Who were the Keystone Kops?
5. In what film did Charlie Chaplin first wear his famous tramp costume?
6. In what film does the hero cook and then eat one of his own boots?
7. Which film does the author think is Buster Keaton's finest film?
8. Which two comedians adapted successfully to sound films?
9. Who made *The Cocoanuts*?

CHAPTER 12

1. Who were: (a) William S. Hart? (b) Tom Mix? (c) Roy Rogers?
2. Who made the most famous Western of all and what was its name?
3. Who made *High Noon* and when?
4. What law increased crime in America?
5. Who were Al Capone and Arnold Rothstein?
6. Name at least two actors who starred in gangster films.
7. What type of films did Busby Berkeley work on at Warner Brothers?
8. Who was the young star in *The Wizard of Oz*?

CHAPTER 13

1. Who made animated films really popular?
2. How many separate drawings were needed to make a ten-minute animated film?
3. Name four Walt Disney characters.
4. Who made Popeye the Sailor films?
5. Who was Olive Oyl?
6. Who are: (*a*) Sylvester and Tweetie Pie? (*b*) Tom and Jerry?
7. What do we mean by 'double exposure'?
8. Who was King Kong?

CHAPTER 14

1. What was the name of the English comedian who went to California in 1913?
2. Name four well-known British films.

CHAPTER 15

1. Give the names of one actor, one director and one film from:
   (*a*) India;   (*b*) Japan.
2. Give the names of film directors from three other countries.

Acknowledgements

The publishers would like to thank the following for permission to reproduce photographs in this book:

Popperfoto for photographs on pages 7, 36, 40 and 41. Mary Evans Picture Library for illustration on p 11. Central Office of Information for *Drifters* (p 31). Paramount Pictures and the National Film Archives for *Modern Times* (p 48). EMI Film Distributors Ltd., for *Murder on the Orient Express* (pp 52, 53 and 54) and *The Ladykillers* (p 82). MGM and the NFA for *Ben Hur* (p 58). Anthony Morris (London) Ltd., and the NFA for *Stagecoach* (p 64). United Artists and the NFA for *The Roaring Twenties* (p 68) and *The Gold Diggers of '33* (p 69). Walt Disney Productions for *Mickey's Circus* (p 73). RKO General Inc., and the NFA for *King Kong* (p 76). Rank Organisation Ltd., for *Great Expectations* (p 80). Connoisseur Films Ltd., for *The Seven Samurai* (p 86), and the National Film Archive for the pictures from the films, *The Great Train Robbery* (pp 12/13), *Birth of a Nation* (p 20), *Battleship Potemkin* (p 46) and the photograph of Florence Lawrence (p 22).